IMAGES
*of America*

# MARCH
# AIR FORCE BASE

TO MASON WITH LOVE.
WE WILL ALWAYS LOOK
BACK ON THIS DAY WITH
FOND MEMORIES.

LOVE,

GRAMS & TATA

Riverside's hard-won Alessandro Aviation Field had been open less than one month when it was renamed March Field on March 20, 1918, in honor of the late Lt. Peyton C. March Jr., son of Gen. Peyton C. March, army chief of staff during World War I. The young pilot died from injuries sustained in a flying accident the month prior to Alessandro's name change. (Courtesy of the March Field Air Museum.)

ON THE COVER: In October 1932, Hollywood starlet Bebe Daniels visited with Lt. Col. Henry "Hap" Arnold and Maj. Carl "Tooey" Spaatz on the newly completed, realigned flight line. In front of the P-12, the trio evokes a time when aviation was still high adventure, novel, dangerous, and for thousands stationed at and associated with March Field, the most compelling thing in the world. (Courtesy of the March Field Air Museum.)

IMAGES
*of America*

# MARCH
# AIR FORCE BASE

William J. Butler

ARCADIA
PUBLISHING

Published by Arcadia Publishing
Charleston, South Carolina

Printed in the United States of America

Library of Congress Control Number: 2009930174

For all general information contact Arcadia Publishing at:
Telephone 843-853-2070
Fax 843-853-0044
E-mail sales@arcadiapublishing.com
For customer service and orders:
Toll-Free 1-888-313-2665

Visit us on the Internet at www.arcadiapublishing.com

*For the airmen and the soldiers: Col. John E. Butler Jr.,
M.Sgt. Jack D. Caraway, T.Sgt. George W. Singer,
Col. Raymond M. Butler, and Col. Arthur M. Butler*

# CONTENTS

# ACKNOWLEDGMENTS

March Air Force Base, today's March Air Reserve Base, is defined as much by its mission and servicemen and women as it is by geography, architecture, and roaring jet engines. I think it is, therefore, most appropriate to thank the thousands of men and women who have served in the past and are currently stationed at March for making the base the most significant air station in the western United States.

All but a handful of the images collected here are from the archives of the March Field Air Museum. Museum director Patricia Korzec generously granted unlimited access to the museum's collections and permission to reproduce these incredible images. Archivist Michelle Sifuentes ably assisted in directing me to the many gems in the museum's possession. Unless otherwise noted, all the images in this work are part of March collections.

The images of sports car racing at March are from the collection of the Riverside International Automotive Museum. Curator Bruce Ward tracked down the evocative images printed here from the collection of photographer Derek Green, who shot the originals. Museum president Doug Magnon generously granted permission to reproduce the rare images.

Flight line safe takeoff efforts were supported by my wonderful mother, Debbie, and prodded by the "old man," my father, Colonel Raymond. My lovely Holly tolerated missed weekends for the months dedicated to producing this book, for which I am thankful.

From start to finish, editor Debbie Seracini provided helpful flight plans through my first publishing experience, subtly willing the wheels off the ground.

# INTRODUCTION

Sixty miles from Los Angeles sits one of the most significant military installations in the United States. Since ground breaking in 1917 at the height of World War I, March Field (today March Air Reserve Base) has fulfilled missions that have come to define the modern air force in peacetime and every major conflict of the 20th century. The base has shaped the landscape and surrounding community of Riverside, California, and has served as both home and workplace to thousands of men and women in uniform and civilian staff from around the world and continues building on its legacy today.

The foundations of March Field were laid upon shaky ground. Even at the height of the international terror and turmoil of the Great War, air combat was largely an unproven and extremely dangerous enterprise. Respected voices in American and European military circles decried aviation in general and military flying in particular as foolish, never to replace the proven, sometimes ancient tactics of the ground war. For their time, they were sometimes right; contemporary military aircraft were winged coffins, dependable neither for offense nor defense in their infancy. Planes clung to the air as little more than box kites with engines.

Fortunately, new voices in combat tactics and practices prevailed upon leaders in Washington and at military headquarters throughout the country. Their resounding call to mount up was adopted by inventors and adventurers who believed in the remarkable and unprecedented possibilities of air combat—and recognized its necessity in the grim face of a global war. The scant decade between the time when the Wright brothers kicked up the sands on a North Carolina beach and the days when the skies were blackened by smoke and gunfire from aerial weapons platforms over France had witnessed incredible strides in technology, but room for improvement was immense. Congress allowed a mere $300,000 for aviation efforts in 1915. A month after the United States declared war on Germany and formally entered World War I in 1917, American legislators invested $640 million for air combat endeavors. The move foreshadowed the resource allowances that would turn the backward air forces of the United States into the absolute world leader in only a few decades.

Amid this rise in spending for air technology and increased interest in its wartime possibilities, Riverside businessmen embarked on a campaign to bring military airpower to Southern California. On the heels of an announcement made in March 1917 by the War Department outlining the need for more and better air installations for America's growing air forces, Arthur N. Sweet, a member of the Riverside Chamber of Commerce and official observer for the local chapter of the Aero Club of America, set about obtaining local interest in making Riverside the location of a new base. Along with a small consortium of prominent local citizens, Sweet offered land and the promise of utilities in Riverside's Alessandro district should the city be selected as the home of the new installation. A telegram from Washington briefly discouraged the hopefuls with its answer, "No . . . the camp would have to be located on the ocean."

Undeterred by the rebuff, Sweet doubled his efforts and enlisted the help of A. S. Dudley, another Riverside Chamber of Commerce officer, and Carl McStay, proponent of improved roadways throughout the country and a representative of the Ocean to Ocean Highway Association of California. Their influence drove the chamber to create a permanent aviation committee with Sweet as chairman. Included on the new committee were Riverside attorneys W. A. Purington and George Sarau; Lt. George Price, ROTC instructor for the local high school and junior college; and perhaps most importantly, Frank A. Miller, owner of Riverside's landmark Mission Inn hotel.

With confidence unfazed by the military's initial resistance to a Riverside site, the men set about organizing a far-reaching campaign of letter writing, local boosterism, and calling of political favors to make the Alessandro tract more attractive for military leaders. Congressmen and military authorities were besieged by the committee's efforts. The work was rewarded with the promise that Riverside was among the sites to be surveyed by a special dispatch from the War Department, due in California in November 1917.

Again their efforts met with failure: Riverside was ranked third in the list of leading sites considered. Tracy and Bakersfield handily beat the city's offers of land and local support. Still, they would not give up their hope that Riverside would play a role in what had clearly become a matter of national survival in a military sense. Air power was here to stay, as each day more and more evidence came from the front lines of the war illustrating the importance of air power and further underscoring the need for investment, training, and increased presence on the home front. The committee aligned itself for a last ditch, do-or-die push to get official support for a Riverside air base.

Congressmen William Kettner, Hiram W. Johnson, James D. Phelan, and Henry Z. Osborne, who represented the whole of the Southern California legislative delegation, received special attention from the committee in order to ensure their support. Their efforts expanded into a full-blown sales kit for the Alessandro site: photographs; aerial and panoramic views; supplemental data on weather, health, water, and moral conditions; and flying situation evidence collected by local aviation expert J. B. Lippincott showing that "30 per cent more flying time could be done in Riverside than in any other part of the country."

The detail efforts worked. In mid-January 1918, a War Department commission spent two days in thorough examination of Riverside's Alessandro tract and surrounding topography. They checked local records on everything from rainfall to health conditions and concluded that "with hardly a tree or a wire to interfere in the flights," the Alessandro site made perfect sense for an aviation training and flight staging installation. The official documents creating Alessandro Aviation Field were signed the evening of January 18. Work was promised to begin within a week, and a small delegation of men was sent to the Alessandro site to begin its transition from dusty fields to an operating air base. The tight initial construction schedule allowed for a mere 90 days in which to construct runways, hangars, barracks, and support structures for the nation's newest combat aviation training center. The contingent of enlisted men sent to the site found the conditions dusty and arid, the landscape flat between rolling, rocky hills. The crew "hoisted a bamboo pole and wind sock," wrote T.Sgt. Glenn Lewis in a 1976 history of the base, "then they spread a long strip of bunting on the ground as a landmark in lieu of a runway."

Little more than a month later, Alessandro Field officially opened on March 1, 1918. A few weeks later, the facility's name was changed to March Field in honor of the late Lt. Peyton C. March Jr., son of Gen. Peyton March, the army's chief of staff during the late stages of World War I. A portrait of the late airman resides in the base headquarters building of 1929, a tribute to the base's namesake and the efforts of March's proponents.

The new installation's efforts to train men to fly air combat missions in World War I were short lived. On November 11, 1918, less than a year after the field opened, the Armistice was signed, putting an end to the first mission assigned to March Field. Subsequent orders kept March active for training purposes for nearly a decade with little change in the infrastructure of the base, save for a few new buildings and updated flight patterns. March closed briefly in 1923 as a training base but continued to be occupied by military staff until its reentry to mainline operation—and expansion—in 1927. Methods and aircraft changed little between the close of the war and 1926, when the U.S. Air Service was renamed the U.S. Army Air Corps and a new program of training for combat readiness was initiated for bases throughout the country. The date also signaled the reopening of March in an accelerated level of importance from its original mandate.

March Field was selected as an installation whose location and past history made it a ripe candidate for expanding pursuit (early tactical fighters) and bomber units meant to bring national air readiness closer to that needed for another full-scale multinational war. In 1927, work began on constructing more permanent buildings for the base in anticipation of its becoming the home of both major bombardment and pursuit units. Its continuing training mission had grown from turning out barely a dozen graduates every four months up through 1920 to several hundred just a decade later when March hit its second stride. In addition to the buildings, new aircraft were assigned to units operating at March, including the P-26 Peashooter, the world's first monoplane pursuit/fighter airplane, and the Martin B-10, the world's first all-metal monoplane bomber.

By early 1934, the new construction phase was complete after an investment of more than a million dollars. Frank Miller's influence on the new buildings was seen in the use of the talents of architects responsible for much of his nearby Mission Inn. The new construction was patterned largely after the same Mission-inspired design of Miller's hotel, from the poured-in-place concrete walls to the red tile roofs and ironwork railings, a move endorsed by officers at March desirous of making the new structures at the base not merely functional but also attractive. Congressman Melvin Maas of St. Paul, Minnesota, gushed that March Field was "destined to be the most beautiful army post in the United States, which means the world as well." A testament to the building methods and classic nature of the design, these buildings continue to function as part of the core of March to this day, as does the line of hangars added in the ambitious construction phase.

The 7th Bomb Group and 11th Bomb Squadron were assigned to March Field in October 1931. A dozen other units followed—the 9th, 22nd, and 31st Bomb Squadrons; the 17th, 34th, 73rd, and 95th Pursuit Squadrons; later the 17th Attack Squadron; and largest and most prestigious of all for the burgeoning aviation powerhouse, the 1st Bomb Wing—bringing with them the forefathers of today's modern Air Force, aircraft and aviators who would come to define the direction and ambition of a nation bent on worldwide air supremacy. Particularly significant is Gen. (then Lt. Col.) Henry "Hap" Arnold's leadership of the base from 1931 to 1936, pivotal years not only in the formation of March and its architectural and design paradigms, but also in the further development of the Army Air Corps itself. Arnold is called the "Father of the Modern Air Force" by historians for his efforts in underscoring the importance of airborne combat ability, and there is little doubt that much of his reputation was sealed during his tenure at March. The officer's club, central to the social lives of airmen and women stationed at the base, is named in Arnold's honor.

In the following decades, March would fulfill its founders' lofty goals to a degree as unimaginable to them as the advances in airpower might have been to the Wright brothers. Through the days leading up to World War II, the Cold War, Desert Storm, and even until today's modern war on terror, March has proven itself equal to the incredible demands of a modern aerial combat facility through presidential administrations, changes in aircraft design, and the varied range of cultural changes in America. Important not only for its contributions to military aviation, March has played an enormous cultural and personal role in the lives of thousands of people stationed there throughout its near-century of service. Bob Hope gave his first true United Service Organizations (USO) show in the March Field gymnasium. As the closest major air base to Hollywood, dozens of films and television shows have used the tarmac and checkerboard-painted hangars of the flight line as backdrops, thousands turned out to see sports cars race on the tarmac during the Cold War, and icons who transcended the lines between aviation fame and popular celebrity—like Amelia Earhart and Charles Lindbergh—visited the base and acknowledged its unique design, utility, and significance.

Through the years—from Alessandro Field, to March Field, March Air Force Base, and now, March Air Reserve Base—March has been forward-facing, ever on the cusp of the cutting edge. Where Curtiss Jenny biplanes once soared are C-17s, the most advanced cargo and transport aircraft in the world. The Fourth Air Force and the 452nd Air Mobility Wing continue the mission outlined in 1918, a promise to protect American interests on the ground by keeping watch from the air. Still the legacy of March is yet to be completed. It is a living base where the propeller days of 1918 echo beside the jets of the modern era. The grandchildren of men and women processed through March on their way to fight in World War II fly from the base to destinations in Iraq, Afghanistan, and a dozen other places where the base acts as a launching point for new examples of the impact of combat aviation—and it is the place where thousands of families are reunited after months of separation. "Its fame is to go far," said Congressman Melvin Maas. "Its marvelous structural features are matched by its location." Those features are matched only, perhaps, by the high quality of the personnel assigned to March, its achievements, and its marvelous story.

# One

# ALESSANDRO AVIATION FIELD
## RIVERSIDE TAKES TO THE AIR
## (1918–1931)

Dusty furrows at the foot of the Box Spring grade were merely the canvas upon which Riverside luminaries lead by Frank A. Miller imagined they might create a modern aviation center for their region. Encompassing portions of the Hendrick Ranch and Alessandro town site, and bisected by the Santa Fe Railroad's right of way, the land where Alessandro Aviation Field would soon rise presented a formidable task to those who would tame it.

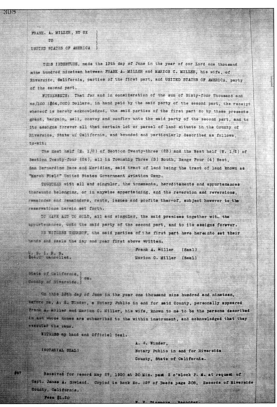

Mission Inn owner Frank A. Miller lent his considerable skills in business ventures to the procurement of land and a plan for a Riverside aviation field. By lending his signature to this deed, Miller effectively gifted the land for a military aviation field to the United States government for a song—just $1 for the first five months and $64,000 for the purchase of all 640 acres of the original plot.

Hired from nearby Colton, a team of muleskinners was employed to help grade the Alessandro site into a proper landing strip. Their arrival signaled the beginning of a whirlwind construction effort to erect service buildings and housing for the permanent staff and cadets set to arrive scarcely a month after construction commenced.

In addition to helping grade the land, the mules used in the early stages of Alessandro's development aided work in laying the foundations of the first buildings. Aside from the Santa Fe Railroad, no major traffic arteries afforded access to the site. The mules were soon employed to remedy this condition by helping to grade working roads within and surrounding the infant airfield.

The view looking down the flight line to the southeast encompasses nearly the entire 1918 base. Hangars, repair and support facilities, barracks, and offices served the burgeoning airfield for two decades before an almost wholesale replacement in the early 1930s.

By July 1918, the renamed March Field was a fully functional aviation center. Likely taken from on board a Curtiss JN-4 Jenny—one of early aviation's leading aircraft—this view shows a row of more than a dozen hangars, a large number of service buildings and base housing, and of utmost importance, the water tower. The olive grove near the bottom of the image is a remnant of the former Hendrick Ranch.

Surrounded by modern equipment inside a repair hangar, these machinists were equal parts expert and innovator, forced to make due with the limited knowledge of aircraft maintenance during aviation's infancy. Little time would pass before the traditional woodcutting devices seen here would make way for updated implements used for shaping metal components.

The "dope and fabric" room (above) of a repair hangar (below) housed canvas and resins used in sheathing the wooden frames of early aircraft. Little more than powered kites, these early aircraft required constant attention on their soft fabric coverings for damage sustained in everyday flight. In the first full year of training flights, planes like the JN-4 Jennys seen here flew in excess of 35,000 hours for a distance of over two-and-a-half million miles.

Early aircraft engines were generally sourced from or based on the design of automobile engines. Before the rise of radial power plants, engines built in the familiar "V" pattern were less efficient and more difficult to cool than their circular offshoots, but at the time this World War I–era photograph was taken, a wider range of mechanics understood their inner workings.

A 1918 auditorium provided both an educational and social space for cadets and base staff at March. Here both would receive briefings about combat zones during the Great War. As a staple of mainline military and aviation-specific institutions, halls such as this would play heavily in the careers of flyers and support staff throughout the 20th century and to the modern day.

Columbus Day, 1918, brought some 103 Curtiss JN-4 Jennys, largely made up of planes from newly opened March Field, over the skies of Los Angeles. There they dropped leaflets reading, "What if we were Germans? Buy Liberty Bonds." It was the most dramatic episode during March's brief tenure as a World War I training facility.

This building appears to be the first base exchange, flanked to the left by the machine shop. To the rear is the engine repair building and a motor pool. March existed as its own community. The exchange was something of the social center of the early base, a meeting spot for the men stationed at March and their families.

This photograph is looking down the 1918 flight line to the northwest. Little more than barns, these early hangars were part of the original 12 built in the initial 60-day construction period of the base, distinguished not only for the completion of a fully operational base in so short a span but also for its achievement as the only such government project completed on schedule up to that point.

From 1918 to 1923, the post headquarters sat beneath one of March Field's two water towers. This building later became the post school and was used in this capacity throughout the mid-1920s and 1930s. Little more than a decade later, it was razed along with much of the original 1918 base.

July 1918 saw the completion of the post bakery, essential to the further health of fledgling March Field. The building lasted long after most other World War I–era buildings were removed and is now the only building remaining from that period. It sits near the location of the officers' pool, which was closed and filled with cement in the mid-1990s.

LINE FOR INSPECTION BY GEN. PEYTON C. MARCH   MARCH 20, 1919.

Precisely one year after opening, March made ready to host the father of its namesake. When Gen. Peyton C. March arrived on March 20, 1919, the base was ready for an inspection on the flight line, marching demonstrations, and a display of evidence showcasing its incredible growth in the space of a single year. The achievement presaged yet more success, though America's involvement in the Great War was nearing an end.

Shipping out to locations far away and mysterious, these airmen board a rail consist on the spur of the Santa Fe Railroad built specifically to service the base. March has been a hub for servicemen and women headed overseas throughout its near-century of existence, beginning just weeks after its March 1918 opening.

Lighter-than-air balloons were a major part of the reconnaissance effort during World War I. Such aircraft were often seen at March during its first year of operation. This view shows one tethered to the ground during a 1920 demonstration day open to citizens in neighboring areas and those who made the trek from Riverside city.

A pair of De Havilland (Airco) DH-4s sits before a powered airship during a demonstration day at March on June 14, 1920. The public interest in all things flying made such events incredibly popular, especially in the pioneering days of military aviation. March continues the tradition with a well-attended annual air show in the present day.

Visitors to the demonstration day could experience an exciting—perhaps frightening—novelty in a balloon ascension. Powered, heavier-than-air flight was little more than a decade old, and the vast majority of Americans had not yet left the ground by any means of powered flight, airplane or balloon.

The De Havilland (Airco) DH-4s were introduced to U.S. air units in early 1918 and were in use by 13 American squadrons by the end of the year. The DH-4 was a versatile airframe and proved valuable in many early combat aviation experiments as well as ably serving in the Great War. They remained in official use by American forces until 1932.

Early March Field had the perfect mixture of then high technology and outright Wild West–style adventure. In the early 1920s, the base was frequently a subject of Los Angeles–area news. Sharp-eyed readers will see "MGM News" written on the side of the camera being used to film a group of mugging flyboys.

The MGM cameras were out to see the new De Havilland (Airco) DH-4M, the ultimate version of the versatile DH-4. (The "M" was for "modernized.") This one, manufactured by Boeing, was equipped with a Liberty L-12 and was built after the war from surplus components originally slated for combat use.

Oddball aircraft passed through March at frequent intervals. On a soggy day at March, in the early part of the 1920s aviation boom, this Loening COA-1 drew a good deal of attention from March airmen and young aviation buffs alike.

Fueling up in the early days was a more casual affair than modern antistatic devices fixed to multi-axle specialized trucks. This 1918 Curtiss JN-4 was the staple trainer for thousands of pilots during World War I and beyond; March used the Jenny well into the 1920s.

Here a De Havilland DH-4 is nose-down on the flight line. Little more than box kites with an engine, early planes like this were very susceptible to the strong and often unpredictable wind patterns of the March landscape, especially at takeoff or landing. The pilot seems to have taken his tumble with admirable calm.

Winds were not the only enemy of safe flight line operations for pilots. A couple of training aircraft seem to be a bit tangled up outside one of the 1918 hangars.

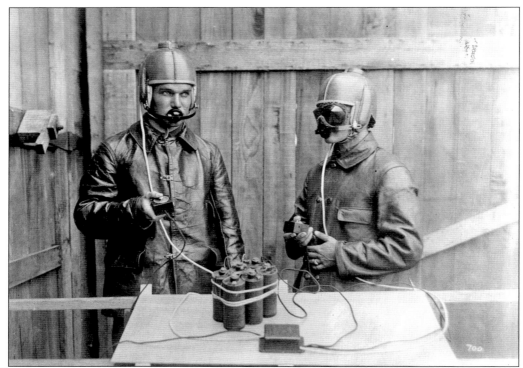

Military fashion tended toward the Buck Rogers futuristic in this early aerial telecommunications test. Early pilots were forced to rely on keen vision rather than radio devices to communicate between themselves. A single-piece headphone receiver and mouthpiece integrated into an all-weather helmet was an innovation developed at March just after the close of World War I.

Perhaps the only drill with guaranteed turnout was the call to the mess hall from 1919 to the modern day. Here airmen line up, plates in hand, to be served from large steaming drums.

Cadets stand outside the flight line operations center—the equivalent of today's air traffic control tower—in 1929. The pilot at front wears the heavily layered uniform required for open-cockpit flying.

Looking north between the lines of 1918 hangars, this cadre of World War I–era airmen appears to be fronted, strangely, by a U.S. Navy officer at the right. Inside the hangar at left, a pair of Jennys await a looking-over. Not one of the structures seen here still stands.

Some things never change—the 1918 need to blow off steam is the same as today's. Shooting dice behind their quarters, these men compare wits—and hats—in order to get in a little fun.

March had a baseball team before it had most tenets of a modern air base. Established in 1920, the team challenged local civilian and military clubs on the diamond, part of an athletic tradition that helped boost morale and gave the base life a touch of home.

A detachment from March en route to the 1919 Tournament of Roses Parade in Pasadena pauses for a photograph on the long, dusty way from Riverside. At an average rate of just under 40 miles per hour on roads crisscrossing the map with little rhyme or reason, the trip from the base to Colorado Boulevard took the better part of a day.

The 311th Aero Squadron is pictured as it appeared in July 1918, just before its redesignation as E Squadron, an alphabetization of all numbered training units at March. A number of the men

The trusty backbone of all military installations around the world is the motor pool, a mishmash of transport, repair, refueling, and emergency vehicles. The March motor pool around 1918 was just that: a collection of workhorses brought in to help build the base initially and kept on to assist daily operations. A close look at the old-fashioned lamps above the engine cowlings gives a clue as to the vehicles' vintages.

seen here found their way to Europe just in time to see the end of World War I.

Two men appear to be repairing the road beside the non-commissioned officer (NCO) barracks, located beside the westernmost water tower, in the summer of 1918.

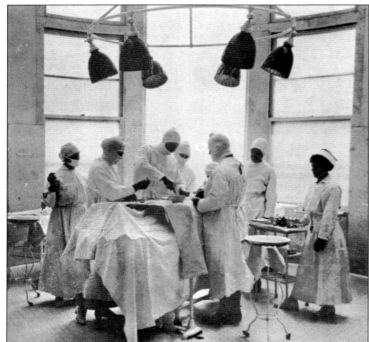

No flight-related deaths were reported for the duration of the Great War at the fledgling March Field, but the same could not be said for those afflicted with the nationwide influenza pandemic. Three March Field personnel died of the disease, including a hospital nurse like the woman seen at far right in this 1919 view.

The base commander's quarters was one of the first structures to be completed in the spring of 1918. The olive grove surrounding the house was original to the Alessandro tract. When the head of construction, Capt. William H. Carruthers, saw the grove, he insisted it be kept as part of the landscaping for the commanding officer's house.

This is the 1928 version of a virtual reality trainer. Based on a type of gyroscopic fly-by-wire interface, early training apparatus like these roughly simulated the mechanical aspects of flying—even, as the cadet below has found out, the hairier moments.

A footnote to the story of early March Field is found in this original 1918 hangar. In 1923, as March was looking forward to a large expansion and new sense of permanency, one of the 1918 hangars was sold to Hemet Union High School, some miles away in Hemet, California. For just $900, the high school got a structure to utilize as a new gymnasium, a building in use until the late 1960s, when at last it was razed.

## *Two*

# WITH FLYING COLORS
## INNOVATIVE AIR TRAINING AT MARCH FIELD
## (1932–1940)

This is March Field in 1936 from 10,000 feet. This was the base of Arnold and Spaatz, the first monoplanes and big bombers, renewed attention from Hollywood for the glamour of the air, and new prestige for a base already intrinsic to America's growing air combat strength. The construction that began in late 1928 is complete. The only reminder of the original March Field is the row of three remaining 1919 hangars at the mid-top right of this view, angled towards the new checkerboard-roofed hangars.

Late in 1928, construction began on a complete reimagining of March Field. Expected to conclude in no more than a year, the construction on the new base—a line of new hangars, barracks, headquarters building, hospital, theater, officer's club, and family housing units—did not finish entirely until 1934. The splendor of what was created, however, earned the dusty landscape seen here the only half-kidding moniker "Green Acres."

Icon of American aviation's golden age, renowned pilot, and one of the most influential personages in the history of American combat aviation, Henry "Hap" Arnold took command at March on November 26, 1931. During his nearly five years as base commander, Arnold led the charge to make an ever-larger, more powerful air corps and, in the meantime, used his considerable charisma and influence to host dozens of eminent officials and celebrities, intending to cement March as the western United States' premiere aviation center. The officer's club was named for him in the 1950s.

Here is a high-angle view of the March bachelor officers' quarters—today's March Inn—under construction in 1929. The swimming pool between the water tower and the quarters remained in service until the late 1990s, when it was unceremoniously filled with cement. The remainder of the wooden buildings were removed shortly after this photograph was taken.

The trees aren't the only new things in this 1934 view of the bachelor officers' garages. The buildings were part of the great base expansion, and remodeling concluded that year, along with lots of landscaping, as evidenced by the furrowed dirt fields in the foreground replaced shortly by lush lawns.

Also completed in 1931 was the new base headquarters building, seen here shortly after with a B-10 flanked by a pair of P-26 Peashooters. Significant things happened there: pivotal decisions by Hap Arnold, visits from Lindbergh and Earhart, reviews from generals and governors, and the passing through of countless airmen on hundreds of missions.

By 1940, an enclosed observation tower had been placed atop the 1934 headquarters building. These were heady, changing days of modern cars in the parking lot and the ultra-modern B-17 seen to the left of the building, which signaled a new era in America's air prowess. A few years hence, this upstart flying force would become the world's greatest.

By the first part of 1932, major construction on March Field's near-complete redesign was finished, although aspects continued until 1934. The central parade grounds—flanked by the new base headquarters (from where this view was photographed), firehouse, barracks, and (at upper right) new hospital—marked the modernization and renewed formalization of the base.

BARRACKS, MARCH FIELD, CALIF.

Beginning in 1931, men were housed in one of two large new barracks buildings constructed as part of the major remodeling of the base begun in 1928. Still standing, these buildings now serve as office space for the ongoing medical missions under Fourth Air Force.

The ability to fill up at a modern gas station was added during March's major expansion. As the base's mission expanded outward beyond only aerial training, families began to make March home. As a result, most of the elements found in a normal city needed to be built on the base to service the large population living there.

Officers' housing in the new Mission-style design directive of March Field was home to thousands of servicemen for 60 years before being turned into civilian housing in the mid-1990s. The neighborhood presaged countless other Southern California housing tracts of the 1930s built in a similar architectural style.

Here a vehicle is checking in at the new main gate in 1934 with a vast dusty field behind it. Although moved from their original 1931 position, the gates and gatehouse still stand on the March of today, just at the entrance to the 1930s neighborhood of base housing across the street from the 1970 chapel.

March Field maintained a lodge at Big Bear Lake, a little more than an hour away in the San Bernardino Mountains. Throughout the 1930s and early 1940s, the lodge served as a retreat for officers and enlisted men alike eager for a respite from the dusty March locale in the cool shade of Big Bear's pines.

(G-297-105NᵀᵀW[2-23)(3-29-32-3-00PM) GOV. JAMES ROLPH JR. AND PARTY AT MARCH FIELD CALIF.

California governor James Rolph (center) dropped in for a base inspection in March 1932. Personally guided by then–Lt. Col. Hap Arnold (head turned to side), Rolph was treated to a banner day: aerial reviews, troop inspections, and a procession around the central parade grounds with marching airmen and an honor band. Rolph inspected lines of Curtiss B-2 Condors during his visit. A full contingent of airpower was showcased on the flight line, in addition to aerial demonstrations, a parade, and thousands of excited guests. Rolph, a former mayor of San Francisco, remains the longest-serving person to fill that office, and the San Francisco–Oakland Bay Bridge is named for him.

(G-300-100NᵀᵀW[2-23)(3-29-32-3 30PM) GUARD OF HONOR FOR GOV. JAMES ROLPH JR. AT M      CALIF.

Looking south onto the newly built structures around the central parade grounds in late 1932 reveals the harmonious design of March Field's second great construction. Immediately on the left side of the street bisecting this view is the base gym where, just a few years after this photograph was taken, Bob Hope would make entertainment history by performing his first radio show for a military audience. The two large structures to the right are the NCO quarters. At top left is the base hospital, with staff quarters to its right.

DRUM & BUGLE CORPS, MARCH FIELD, CALIF.

The March Drum and Bugle Corps of 1934 drill outside the base headquarters building. Ceremonial music was integral to the operations life of March Field. The balcony behind the band held hundreds of dignitaries throughout the 1930s, the golden age of aviation, all hosted with musical pomp.

Part of the 1928–1934 remodeling and major expansion of March included construction of a well-appointed movie theater on the parade grounds. There, leading films of the day, newsreels, cartoons, comedy short subjects, and documentaries matched the programming in civilian theaters, as seen in these schedules from 1933.

The Post Theatre, or War Department Theatre, in 1934 was a jewel in the crown of the Mission Inn–inspired design of the remodeled base. Inside, details like plaster molding, colorful paint schemes on the ceiling and borders, and custom lighting fixtures made the theater the centerpiece of a showplace base. Today it serves as the Cultural Center, home to many formal ceremonies like promotions and retirements.

This photograph was taken after a show on a cool night in the early 1930s. The theater served a dual purpose: entertaining the troops and keeping them on base away from civilian delights. March was its own city, and the theater was the center of culture on most nights throughout the year.

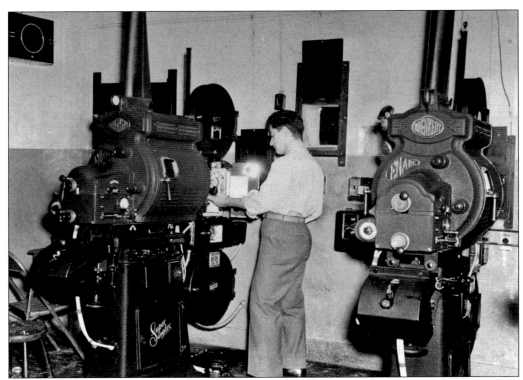

This photograph is taken of the projection booth around 1934. The theater was one of the first buildings at March to feature air-conditioning. The projection booth, however, received little of the cooling benefits—the projectionist's rolled-up sleeves give it away.

**Non-Commissioned Officers' Club**

*March Field, California*

Umnitz, Fred A.  M/Sgt.

*is a member of the N. C. O. Club in good standing and is entitled to all privileges of the Club.*

This Card must be presented for admission to all functions of the Club.

R. Coulter                M. Peterson
PRESIDENT        SECRETARY & TREASURER

Second to the base theater for social culture were the clubs for officers and non-commissioned officers. This membership card belonging to M.Sgt. Fred A. Umnitz guaranteed socials, dances, dinners, and drinks with fellow airmen and even "dames," all important structures in military life now and then.

The newly built officer's club matches the rest of March's new Mission-influenced architecture. Essentially a private club where pilots could cool down, the officer's club retained its feeling of aerial bonhomie for nearly 60 years before it was consolidated with the non-commissioned officer's club and modernized into a more standard neighborhood-style bar.

This postcard shows inside the well-appointed officer's club, with space for games, reading, and relaxing with a stiff drink after too much time behind the stick. Exuding masculinity, the 1943 club building was right in line with traditional, dark-wood clubs found on bases throughout the nation. Later named for Gen. Hap Arnold, the club retains a feel similar to this late-1930s view.

Long before direct-deposit, airmen had to line up en masse to claim their pay. In 1938, enlisted men and officers alike wait their turn outside the paymaster's quarters—an average of $18 a week for pilots.

The 34th Attack (Pursuit) Squadron was home to the venerable Boeing P-26 Peashooter, among other early tactical fighter aircraft. The 34th headquarters building was part of the newly remodeled base's construction and served throughout the 1930s and into the World War II era.

Actor Wallace Beery visited March in the early 1930s, perhaps to promote his 1931 film *Hell Divers*, starring Beery and Clark Gable. Beery played both U.S. Air Corps and Navy officers in a number of films throughout his distinguished career, which began with silent films in 1913.

One aircraft of the early-1930s 31st Bomb Squadron was the open-cockpit B-4, the star of a film whose aerial scenes were shot at March. Here actors and studio officers pose in front of the massive B-4 some time in 1931.

Actress Rochelle Hudson graced March Field with a visit in November 1936. Standing before a Martin B-10, Gen. Delos C. Emmons pinned a pair of aviator's wings onto the actress's lapel in addition to lending her an iconic flight cap with air corps wings.

Hollywood types and March officers pose on the wings and in front of a Curtiss B-2 Condor. A dozen films were made using aircraft from March Field during the 1930s. The new buildings erected between 1928 and 1934 provided a glamorous backdrop equal to the thoroughly modern lines of the airplanes stationed there and were popular both in entertainment and newsreels.

"I can't quit . . . I'm a test pilot," said Clark Gable in the 1938 film *Test Pilot*, shot on location at March Field in 1937. Also starring Hollywood legends Spencer Tracy, Myrna Loy, and Lionel Barrymore, the film utilized March's new B-17s, then the Air Corps' newest and most sophisticated bombers. Although largely forgotten today, *Test Pilot* was purportedly Myrna Loy's personal favorite of all her films.

An air show in 1935 showcased the newly completed March Field modernization and remodeling and gave the base a chance to show off its aerial prowess. Parachutists make a daring leap over the flight line from a C-14, thrilling the large crowd assembled below.

The brand new flight line is shown in full fig, crowded with airplanes out for concentrated maneuvers in 1933. Bombers and observation, pursuit, and transport airplanes fill the entirety of the ramps alongside the new hangars, a sure sign that March had broken away from its dusty, unsure beginnings to become a base meriting attention and respect.

Large crowds turned out for the flight demonstration presented when Governor Rolph came to town in March 1932. Enormous Keystone bombers and spindly P-12s took to the sky to the thrill of the spectators standing alongside the thoroughly modern flight facilities completed hardly a year before.

This is an image of sightseeing with the Keystone B-4s on approach into March Field. Local landmarks are identified in mountains to the north and west. Right ahead is March Field in its remodeled early-1932 splendor.

This season's greetings picture from the pilot's point of view was taken in 1938. March Field as it existed in its first two decades is almost entirely gone, replaced by the new master-planned, modern base. Only two of the original 1918 hangars remain, located directly beneath the second "E" in "greetings."

The Christmas season of 1929 saw the old March Field making way for the new. Here, the line of new hangars is complete, as are the barracks and new headquarters building. Missing still is any sign of landscaping, the base hospital, theater, chapel, and numerous other support buildings.

The Caterpillar Club was so called because of the silk parachutes of the members who jumped, under duress or not, from planes of the 95th Pursuit Squadron, part of the 1st Bomb Wing.

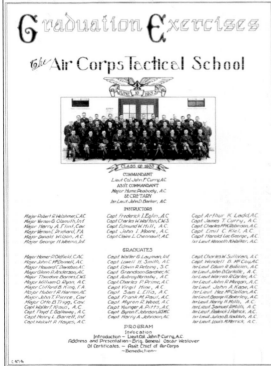

Treated like a college graduation, the commencement exercises for March tactical school cadets were not without the pomp seen in civilian ceremonies. Even in 1933, the airman's job was as dangerous as it had been nearly two decades before during aviation's infancy. Ongoing strides in aviation technology and tactics required constant training, and March was at the center of learning.

Maj. Carl Spaatz (third from left) and Arnold (fourth from left) pose with airmen outside one of the new hangars sometime in the mid-1930s. "He was one of those guys who was spick and span and he always went by the book," a private stationed at March in the early 1930s recalled about Major Spaatz. "When he inspected the troops he went around with a big grin on his face and would chew you out and he really enjoyed it."

Striking a pose on the roof of the headquarters building, these rakish pilots embody the spirit of March and the golden age of aviation. The lines of Boeing P-12s in the background belonged to the 17th Pursuit Group, the planes soon to be replaced by the monoplane P-26 in 1934–1935.

With eyes pointed upward, then–Lt. Col. Hap Arnold and visiting aviatrix Amelia Earhart (both center on the second-floor balcony) study an aerial review during Earhart's 1932 visit to March Field. Already famous throughout the world for her remarkable aviation prowess, Earhart visited the base to meet with Arnold and inspect his command's impressive collection of aircraft and flying units.

Then–Lt. Col. Hap Arnold officiates a pass-in-review march on the flight line some time in the mid-1930s. For all that March had modernized in the years between 1918 and when this photograph was taken, the landscape west of the flight line remained open from horizon to horizon.

Reveille outside the new headquarters building, on the west side of the parade grounds in the early 1930s, officially calls to duty for the day those at March Field. Beyond the honor guard, the lush lawns are augmented by newly planted palm trees, greenery offset by the Spanish-inspired red roofs of the new buildings.

Maj. Gen. Oscar Westover (behind the table, far left in the second row) addresses the 19th Bomb Group on the lawn in front of the headquarters building on September 21, 1938. As chief of the U.S. Air Corps, Westover was responsible for promoting the merits of a larger, better trained air force. Sadly he was killed in a plane crash the same day this photograph was taken while attempting to land in Burbank, California.

Brazilian chief of staff Gen. Goes Monteiro made a point of seeing March Field during a visit in June 1939. Favored for its outstanding location and impressive facilities, March was often placed on the list of must-sees for visiting officials from both the military and civilian sectors touring the western United States. The Brazilian general and his staff were treated to a flight line pass-in-review and aerial demonstrations.

(G257-109I-23)(4-I535-8-30A) MAJ. GEN. MALONE REVIEWING 1ST WING, MARCH FIELD, CALIF.

All the senior officers seen here, including Arnold (foreground, touching the rail) and Major General Malone (to Arnold's right), 9th Corps area commander, and senior staff standing behind them reviewing the 1st Bomb Wing in April 1935, were born in the 19th century. Standing on the second-story balcony of the headquarters building, overlooking the flight line, they witnessed a display impossible only three decades before. The two-day long maneuvers they witnessed were the largest theretofore enacted at March under the new 1st Bombardment Wing.

Baseball continued to play a role at March throughout the 1930s. A new diamond and backstop were built just behind the northernmost barracks in the new construction and were decorated with the insignias of the tactical and bomb groups present at March in the 1930s.

Base housing built between 1932 and the 1941 base expansion was similar to many Southern California neighborhoods, albeit a little closer to serious airpower a couple thousand yards away on the flight line.

P-12s are serviced outside the new hangars in 1931 in front of a hangar where a Curtiss Condor waits in the shadows. The two wheels at the rear of the P-12s made them moveable by a single person—they weighed only 2,600 pounds loaded.

A Keystone B-4 was used as an Army Air Mail plane around 1934. This aircraft made regular stops at a number of Southern California air stations, including March Field. The exposed, elevated cockpit and enclosed payload area made the B-4 an ideal mail carrier.

Every payday, one of the Curtiss B-2 Condors, seen at the rear of this 1931 view, would fly escort to a ground convoy sent to pick up the payroll at a bank in downtown Riverside. In front, the P-12s are being prepared for flight—looking closely reveals pilots at the side of their mounts, ready to take to the air.

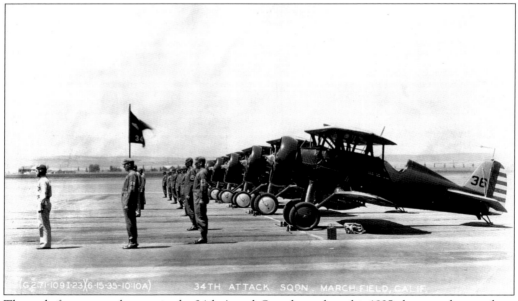

The end of an era can be seen in the 34th Attack Squadron when this 1935 photograph was taken. The monoplane P-26 would replace the biplane P-12s later in 1935, which were in turn replaced by the relatively advanced P-36 before the close of the decade. The 34th would later lend men to aircrews participating in Gen. Jimmy Doolittle's Tokyo Raid.

Taken from the roof of one of the original 1918 hangars, the training aircraft lined up below were rapidly becoming obsolete in this 1929 or 1930 view. March training cadets were used to learning on some of the older equipment. By the close of the 1930s, many of the newer cadets were training in planes older than they were.

(G258-1091-23)(4-15-35-8:15A) 1ST WING G.H.Q. AIR FORCE, MARCH FIELD, CALIF.

Rows of glinting, humming P-26 Peashooters line up on the ramp shortly after their introduction to March Field. Part of the 34th, 73rd, and 95th Pursuit Squadrons, the Peashooters were the most modern aircraft at March when introduced. The last fighter designed with an open cockpit, fixed landing gear, and externally braced wings, the P-26 was also the first such plane fitted with wing flaps to increase drag for landings.

Maj. Clarence Tinker puts a new P-26 through its paces in June 1934. Tracing his ancestry to the Osage Indian tribe, Tinker was well-liked by those under his command and was promoted to major general during World War II. Tinker was killed during the Japanese attack on Midway Island in June 1942 and was posthumously honored by the naming of Oklahoma City's Tinker Air Force Base.

Gleaming P-26 Peashooters sit outside a hangar on March Field's fight line in the mid-1930s. Many of the airplanes seen here were later transferred to the Panama Canal Zone after their replacement P-36s arrived at March. Some of the planes sent to the Panama Canal Zone were sent to the Philippines just before the attack on Pearl Harbor, with most of the 28 stationed there destroyed on the ground by Japanese bombs in early 1941. Only a handful of the airplanes survive today.-

The Martin B-10 entered service in June 1934. Remarkable for being the first all-metal monoplane introduced to regular use, the B-10 was also the first to feature a powered, rotating gun turret and, less flashy but of great importance, the first bomber to feature retractable landing gear. With performance as impressive as the air corps' attack and pursuit aircraft, Hap Arnold called the B-10 an "air-power wonder."

Ordnance is loaded onto the wing-mounted bracket of a Martin B-10 around 1935. Part of the 19th Bomb Group, the B-10s were valuable mostly for their bridging the gap between old and new, replaced for performance and capabilities only when the venerable B-17 was introduced later in the decade.

A pictogram of the airborne sort is in this case a slow and steady transport aircraft probably from the 31st Bombardment Group, part of the 7th Bomb Wing. With a little illustrating skill, members of air units could be immortalized in the insignia of their group, at least until a better artist was found.

The insignia of the 32nd Bombardment Squadron is presented by a Mr. Hutchings (third from left) to Capt. W. O. Eareckson (second from left) in the company of designer Paul Preston (far left) and Col. J. H. Pirie, commander of March Field, in April 1938. The 32nd was a distinguished bomb unit throughout World War II and the Korean Conflict.

TACTICAL TRAINING FLIGHT, 11ᵀᴴ BOMBARDMENT SQUADRON, YOSEMITE VALLEY CALIF.
(O-988-74NJ W)2-23(6-8-32-9-45AM)(12-10200)1W EL-CAPITAN-INSPIRATION POINT-YOSEMITE NATIONAL PARK CALIF.

B-2 Condors from March Field cruise past El Capitan in the Yosemite Valley on a long-distance training flight in June 1932. Long indeed: cruising speed for the Condor was only 114 miles per hour; the open cockpit limited the service ceiling to just over 16,000 feet.

Keystone B-4s cast shadows on the tarmac during Gov. James Rolph Jr.'s visit to March Field in March 1932. They were the last biplane bombers delivered to the Army Air Corps before the all-metal B-10 monoplane signaled the end of the large-scale military biplane for good.

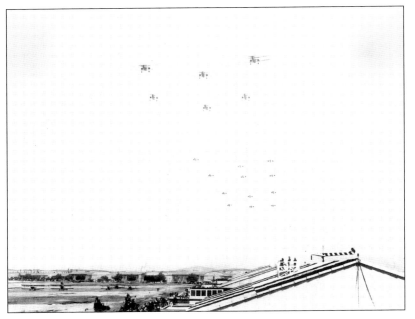

This angle, looking up toward the sky, is seen from the roof of one of the new 1931 hangars. In the distance, three of the original 1918 hangars sit, lingering reminders of the heady days of the past. They would remain well into the 1950s.

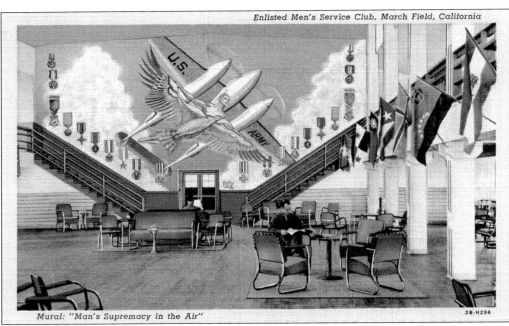

Enlisted Men's Service Club, March Field, California

Mural: "Man's Supremacy in the Air"

The two-story *Man's Supremacy in the Air* mural at the service club was unveiled February 1, 1943. Painted by S.Sgts. Richard Pafferie and Lawrence Colwell, the mural faced the central great room, where airmen found recreational amenities intended to ease wartime stress: game rooms, a cafeteria, and a library, among other offerings.

# *Three*

# MARCH TO WAR
## AIR SUPREMACY FROM RIVERSIDE
## (1941–1945)

HENRY H. ARNOLD
*Major General*
CHIEF OF THE ARMY AIR FORCES

By the start of World War II, Henry "Hap" Arnold had left March, been promoted to major general, and served as the chief of the Army Air Forces. His contributions to March Field were immeasurably valuable; his fingerprints were everywhere on the base. "If I had realized then that I would stay in Washington for ten consecutive years," he would later write of his tenure post-March, "I would almost have dared to turn my overloaded car around and drive straight back to California."

**AIR BASE HEADQUARTERS**
Office of the Commanding General
March Field, Riverside, California

September 2, 1941.

TO: All Members of the March Field Air Base Command:

    With an outstanding record of achievement, March Field stands today with opportunity to gain added laurels in a new field of endeavor. Through years, as the great west coast army pilot training center and later, as the base for forming the First Bombardment Wing, new records for safety and perfection of training were gained by this station.

    Now designated as a Pursuit Base and Wing, we are entering a completely different phase of training. The majority of the officers and men of this command, due to heavy recent enlistments or to having but lately arrived from other stations, are new to the Air Corps.

    Without the obstacle of binding precedent to overcome, I believe that with all members of this command working toward a high state of physical and mental well-being, a state of preparedness second to none can and will be achieved at March Field.

B. G. WEIR
Colonel Air Corps, U. S. Army
Commanding

This letter was written a scant three months before America was forever changed by the attack on Pearl Harbor. In it, Army Air Corps commander B. G. Weir applauds March's personnel for their training efforts, promising at last that "a state of preparedness second to none can and will be achieved at March Field." Scarcely anywhere have words been proven as true so soon.

By September 1941, March was running seriously short of facilities to house its growing staff. Fourth Air Force headquarters was set up in the Virginia Building in downtown Riverside, near the Mission Inn, where it remained for a number of years as expansion at March included absorption of 625 additional acres and Works Progress Administration (WPA) funding to construct new facilities.

G 383G-109I-32AB)(10-27-41) OFFICERS, HEADQUARTERS, FOURTH AIR FORCE, RIVERSIDE, CAL.

Two months before the United States would enter World War II, the staff of Fourth Air Force headquarters in the downtown Riverside annex posed for this rather somber photograph. In just weeks, the entire mission of the unit would change, its outlook forever altered by the grim specter of war.

A sign for the Works Progress Administration work program advertised "March Field Improvements" beyond the southeast gate in April 1940. March employed WPA labor throughout the war years in addition to giving and receiving aid from the Civilian Conservation Corps (CCC). Increased traffic at the base forced the construction of a new road along the western side of the base. The road was surveyed and constructed entirely by the WPA.

In late November 1940, the *March Post Beacon* revealed plans for an antiaircraft artillery camp across the Perris Highway from March Field. Camp Haan, as it would come to be called, would house a hospital, administration buildings, and mess halls, in addition to its field training facilities, with a contingent of 85,000 men at the height of its use. This World War II–era view shows soldiers training in a heavy artillery dugout on a rotating antiaircraft gun.

A souvenir from the war years at March Field, this particular example found its way from March to Illinois and back again. The story is not unlikely: imagine the thousands of matchbooks taken from the base and disbursed by the multitudes of visitors and airmen stationed there over the decades.

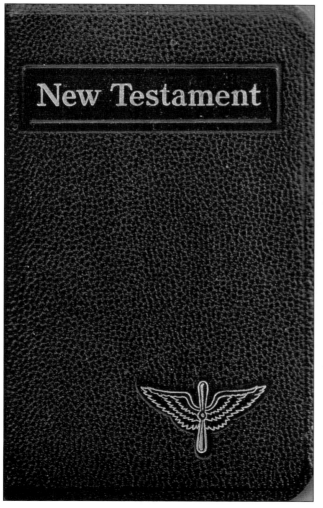

Before pilots were sent overseas from March, they were given a number of kit items like phrasebooks and cloth documents printed in multiple languages to be shared with captors in case of a crash behind enemy lines. Perhaps closest to pilots' hearts were the airmen's bibles, with a foreword by Pres. Franklin Roosevelt. This one was given to the author's grandfather before his deployment to the Pacific theater, where he was to pilot B-25 Mitchells and A-26 Invaders.

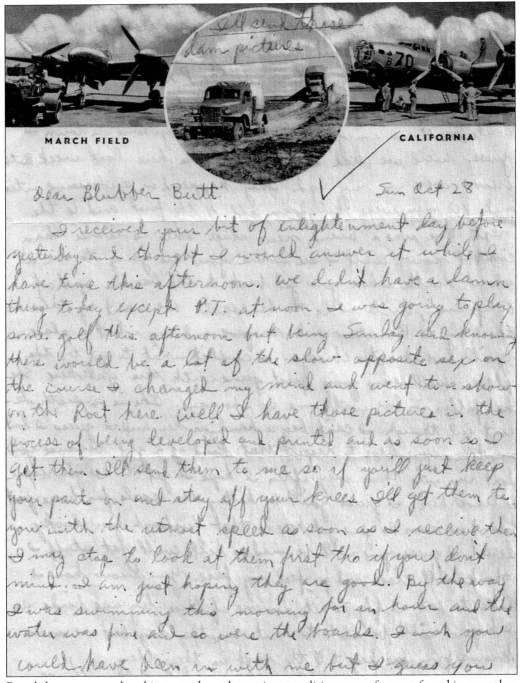

*I'll send these dam pictures*

**MARCH FIELD**    **CALIFORNIA**

Dear Blubber Butt:                                    Sun Oct 28

I received your bit of enlightenment day before yesterday and thought I would answer it while I have time this afternoon. We didn't have a damn thing today except P.T. at noon. I was going to play some golf this afternoon but being Sunday and knowing there would be a lot of the slow opposite sex on the course I changed my mind and went to a show on the Post here. Well I have those pictures in the process of being developed and printed and as soon as I get them I'll send them to me so if you'll just keep your pants on and stay off your knees I'll get them to you with the utmost speed as soon as I receive them. I may stop to look at them first tho if you don't mind. I am just hoping they are good. By the way I was swimming this morning for an hour and the water was fine and so were the boards. I wish you could have been in with me but I guess you

Rough language, crude subjects, and tough wartime conditions were features found in countless letters generated by servicemen throughout the ages. This World War II–era letter from March Field has it all: "Dear Blubber Butt," it reads, "well I have those pictures in the process of being developed." Letters such as this are prized for their first-hand accounts of experiences impossible to otherwise recount. (Courtesy of the author.)

Edgar Bergen (left) and his iconic character Charlie McCarthy visited March as part of a USO contingent during the war. Charlie, with typical deadpan, accepted an honorary commission in the U.S. Army Air Corps. Bergen and McCarthy first appeared during wartime at March at a Christmas show in the base gymnasium just weeks after the attack on Pearl Harbor.

"It's so easy to say pet names when you listen to the trumpet." The anthem of millions from the Big Band era, these lyrics from Stillman and McGrane's "Jukebox Saturday Night" (recorded by Glenn Miller) forever enshrine the trumpet prowess of Harry James, who performed at March in the midst of World War II.

Red Skelton cracked them up at the base gym in the early days of the war, one in a line of comedy greats to grace the same stage, like Jimmy Durante, Desi Arnaz, Victor Borge, George Burns and Gracie Allen, Groucho Marx, and many others.

Jack Benny brought his unique humor and timing to March Field in February 1944, getting laughs along with a little help from a mop-wigged airman. Benny came to perform his weekly radio show at the base—note the microphone to his right.

Joe E. Brown lit up March Field with his trademark smile during a troop visit in the early 1940s. Brown was a well-known USO entertainer during World War II, likely influenced by the loss of his son, Capt. Don E. Brown, in an airplane crash near Palm Springs in 1941. Prior to the war, Brown adopted two German Jewish refugee boys in an effort to spur support for displaced young people in Nazi-overrun Europe.

Bob Hope is second only to Hap Arnold and Curtis LeMay as the patron saint of March Field. Hope recorded many radio shows live at the base, and performed his very first USO show in the base gym in May 1941. Throughout his long and distinguished career, Hope performed at March dozens of times, was part of golf events at the base links (located a little off March proper), and imprinted his iconic image and love for servicemen on the thousands who saw him there.

Just behind the firehouse, right across the street from the flight line, the little March Field Sub-Exchange whetted the whistles and satisfied the hunger of servicemen hard at work in the hangars and support buildings that kept the March contingent of fighters and bombers airworthy during the war years.

A bowling alley was among the most highly requested facilities as March Field continued to expand its entertainment offerings. With the rise in popularity of bowling during the early 1940s, March answered the airmen's call for their own alley by building a state-of-the-art facility shortly after the outbreak of World War II.

Women Air Force Service Pilots (WASPs) stand in formation on the parade grounds. The first WASP arrived at March in January 1944, followed by 26 permanent assignments and dozens more women stationed there temporarily for training.

Arriving at March Field in April 1943, the first women assigned to the base as part of the Women's Army Auxiliary Corps (WAACs) divided into a headquarters and photography unit. At first, the new female contingent was used only in secretarial capacities, but by the end of the war, they were working alongside the men maintaining combat-ready aircraft.

Interesting most for its surreal value, this Christmas 1941 menu from the 32nd Air Base Group at March features a P-40 Warhawk in flight. About the same time these items were printed, real planes like the one illustrated gave chase to Japanese dive-bombers furiously attacking Pearl Harbor, Hawaii.

**43rd & 44th Materiel Squadrons**

32nd Air Base Group

MARCH FIELD, CALIFORNIA

*Merry Christmas*

December 25, 1941

MARCH FIELD, August 1941. Capt. (now Gen.) Boushey's flight in this rocket-assisted Ercoupe was milestone in JPL's development of JATO. Clark Milliken pilots Porterhouse plane in unassisted takeoff from simultaneous start (lower right).

Illustrating the incredible thrust of rockets in a rather dramatic way, this August 1941 experiment used two aircraft beginning takeoff maneuvers simultaneously. While the rocket-assisted aircraft is well airborne, the wheels of the propeller-only powered plane have yet to leave the ground.

In June 1941, an aerial behemoth made its way to March for extensive testing, lasting until December 5 of that year. The Douglas B-19 was the largest aircraft in the world when it appeared at March to complete some 43 hours of in-flight testing. At one point, the enormous plane lifted 17 tons of bombs into the air, bringing the total weight of the loaded aircraft to 70 tons. (Courtesy of the author.)

The incredible size of the B-19 proved far more interesting to contemporary observers than its military capabilities. The image of the young couple in civilian clothes posing with a B-19 wheel and tire assembly is particularly striking. With a crew of 18, a length of 132 feet, a 212-foot wingspan, and topping out at 42 feet tall, the B-19 was a giant indeed, the largest aircraft built for the U.S. Army Air Forces until 1946. (Courtesy of the author.)

Very early pre-production B-17s received a bit of the Southern California touch when these Motorglide scooters were added to aircraft flown from March in 1939 en route to Langley Field, Virginia. One of the little, zippy scooters was loaded into each of the planes; none made it into the production models.

THE B-17-B. NEWEST MODEL OF THE BOEING FLYING FORTRESS. STATIONED AT MARCH FIELD

Although B-17s were introduced to March late in the 1930s, the landmark aircraft was well used throughout World War II. A large number was assigned to March as part of the 17th Attack Group, a unit whose mission was changed to that of a bomber unit in late 1939.

DOUGLAS B-18-A BOMBERS AT MARCH FIELD, CALIF.

B-18s on maneuvers from Hamilton Field's 11 Bomb Squadron in May 1936 await pilots in front of the new hangars. Similar to the B-17 in concept, mission, and even overall design, the B-18 eventually lost out to the B-17 in performance capability and mission utility. (Courtesy of the author.)

The Northtrop A-17 came to March Field's 17th Attack Group in 1935. A thoroughly modern airplane by 1930s standards, the A-17 was a swift attack bomber. Even the pilots began to look more modern, as these men from the 34th Attack Squadron show.

(G-507-1091-23)(10-20-36)    COMBAT CREWS,    34TH ATTACK SQDN., MARCH FIELD, CALIF.

P-38 "Lightenings" Starting to Peel Off, March Field, California

3B-H300

The XP-38 made its maiden test flights at March Field in January 1939. America's first twin-engine fighter, the XP-38 (later designated the P-38) was a top-secret affair, then the world's most cutting-edge aircraft. During World War II, the Lightning, as the P-38 was called for its remarkable swiftness, proved its worth in the European and North African campaigns. Note the similarity between the P-38 seen flying above the group watching the awarding of the Distinguished Flying Cross in front of the base hospital and that in the middle of the previous image.

Troops at Attention on Reviewing Grounds, Station Hospital in Background,

March Field, California, Officer being Awarded a D. F. C.

3B-H302

The P-40 Warhawk, the ultimate development from the highly praised P-36, came to March just after the war began. Much more modern than any fighter or attack plane theretofore stationed at March, the Warhawks presaged nearly all fighter aircraft development until they were supplanted by jet-engined designs toward the end of the war.

The Fourth Air Force's medical department manned the base hospital built as part of the major base remodeling of 1928–1934. Thousands of airmen received their inoculations in the hospital before heading overseas to combat zones. After the war, the families who joined them in Europe or Asia as part of the occupation forces passed through the hospital, too, including the author's father. The building is widely reported to be haunted.

# *Four*

# A CHILL IN THE AIR
## MARCH AIR FORCE BASE IN THE COLD WAR
## (1946–1990)

The Cold War is a memory armed with a double-edged sword for many old enough to remember the period. The peace following World War II saturated the United States with unprecedented plenty, while the grim specter of increasing Soviet strength and influence threatened an outbreak of a new and terrifying war. Renamed March Air Force Base in 1947, the base took part in both elements of the postwar American lifestyle, first as a Tactical Air Command base and later part of Strategic Air Command (SAC). The post exchange, rebuilt in 1932 on the new parade grounds, provides a wonderful example of the lighter, capitalist side of the Cold War.

More than simply a place to shop for home necessities and novelties, the exchange was also the main source for uniforms and uniform devices. As seen in 1947, ties, shirts, long coats, and dress jackets were available for officers and enlisted men alike.

Spendthrifts beware: March's post exchange was nearly as well stocked as any civilian emporium and twice the value because shoppers paid no sales tax. Housewares; jewelry; the latest fashions for men, women, and children; sporting goods; toys; and a wide array of other items were brightly displayed in a way that might make one forget nuclear-weapon-laden aircraft making round-the-clock flights just a few hundred yards away on the flight line. Interestingly, the exchange was one of the few places where hats, apparently, were allowed to be worn indoors.

Post exchange shoppers could also relax at the buffet-style cafeteria for a Coke and a sandwich, prepared and served by the rather grim-looking crew behind the counter. The cafeteria was open to both military and civilian personnel working at March, allowing for mixing in the large, open dining room.

More happening was the lunch counter in another part of the exchange. There young couples and kids sat arm-to-arm at the long counter to enjoy cheap and plentiful food washed down with icy Coke, a national addiction begun in the throes of World War II.

Forget what's playing, the theater is air-conditioned! A warm day in the late 1940s reflects the real attraction of the theater in summer.

A little 1950s snack stand—the Oasis—like the thousands that popped up all over Southern California in the early days of the Cold War, popped up on a corner of the recreational area behind the parade grounds.

Exciting coming events and good deals on dinner were major attractions for the March NCO Club around 1967. The club was the center of social life on base for the noncommissioned officers of its membership. Entertainment and good, cheap food made the club an attractive alternative to going off base.

Staff cars at March were marked with special plates to identify them as government property. This collection of identification plates traces the history of the March motor pool from the hexagonal World War I–era examples to modern, standard license plate–style designs of the 1940s and 1950s.

Competition on the gridiron made for good fun in rivalries between teams from different bases. The March Field Flyers football team had been around since at least 1936. Coached in their December 10, 1944, match by Capt. Paul Schissler, the Flyers were made up of enlisted airmen stationed at the base. The parade grounds of the base served equally well for scrimmages.

OFFICIAL
PROGRAM

Los Angeles Coliseum
December 10, 1944

**RANDOLPH FIELD RAMBLERS vs. MARCH FIELD FLYERS**

5.244 Selling Price
.006 Sales Tax
TOTAL PRICE

**25c**

ORANGE EMPIRE
# NATIONAL SPORTS CAR RACES

50¢

SOUVENIR PROGRAM
NOVEMBER 8, 1953

12266

30

MARCH AIR FORCE BASE, CALIFORNIA

In 1952, Strategic Air Command (SAC) commander Gen. Curtis LeMay opened selected air bases throughout the United States to Sports Car Club of America (SCCA) organizations to hold races on base flight lines. LeMay was himself a sports car fan and drove a Cadillac-powered Allard in the early 1950s. Although wildly popular with race fans—tens of thousands of spectators turned out for races on any given weekend—the races cost the U.S. government a great deal of money. The map of the March track reveals that designers used the long, smooth runway to good advantage in the track's 3.5-mile length during races hosted in November 1953 and 1954. By 1955, the cash-conscious powers shut down the races for good. (Both courtesy of the collection of the Riverside International Automotive Museum.)

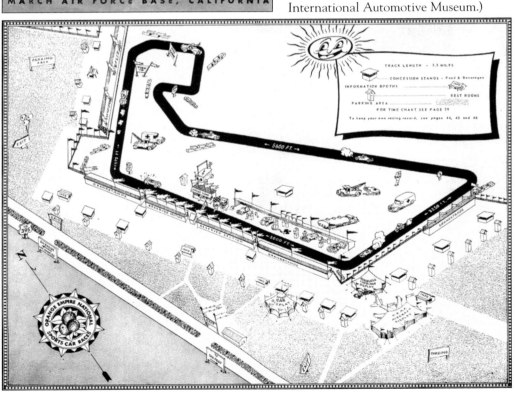

The rows of B-47s providing a backdrop for the Ferraris and crowds reveal that this is no ordinary race track. For a brief time in the early 1950s, the national mania surrounding sports car racing prompted the opening of a number of air bases' runways to weekend racers and privateer teams. Note the chevron on the sleeve of the airman lending a hand to position the Kurtis racer below. The march races remain some of the most seminal of the sports car racing glory days. (Photographs by Derek Green; both courtesy of the collection of the Riverside International Automotive Museum.)

The old runways of the 1930s just couldn't support the enormous long-range bombers of the Cold War. Shortly after the close of World War II, as March was positioned to play a crucial role in heavy bomber missions, new, larger runways were necessary to support the larger aircraft, like the Boeing B-29 and B-47, and later the venerable B-52.

Like other functional cities of 10,000 persons or more, March had a large and well-trained fire department. Essential not only for buildings but for flight-line emergencies, the fire department had been part of the base since the beginning and continues to be housed in this 1931 building today.

Staff of what looks to be a temporary March Air Force Base headquarters building pose outside around 1949. The fluctuating size of the base—from a wartime high of 75,000—and the need to remodel most of the 1930s buildings to support modern missions forced the temporary removal of many offices during this period.

The little train station on the Santa Fe March spur was the site of many arrivals to and departures from March during its many years of service: from just after the base was opened in 1918 to its disuse beginning in the early 1980s. Beloved for its classic station design, the little building was burned to the ground by vagrants after the building and the rail spur were abandoned.

Cutting-edge jet aircraft introduced during the Cold War required new infrastructure on the March flight line. Growth in the 1960s forced the need for a new fuel center to service the large number of long-range bomber, refueling, and transport aircraft stationed at the base during the pivotal era in U.S. Air Force history.

The morning fog lends an ominous touch to an image captured during a readiness exercise sometime in 1956. Although on "yellow alert," the radiation reminder is simply part of the game, one aspect of the constant vigilance required by Cold War nerves.

The old 1932 commissary building was getting a bit dated, not to mention far too small, by the close of the 1970s. A replacement was built far from the center of the 1930s core of the base. The commissary was joined by other new services in the new exchange building, chapel, recreation facilities, and modernized base theater. Because of realignments, changes in command, and overall shifts in mission, only the exchange remains in operation—the commissary has moved yet again.

Airmen are loading a payload into the belly of the BUFF in this 1974 photograph. As a SAC base, March was assigned round-the-clock missions for a number of years during the height of the Cold War. B-52s like this one were in the air around American sectors at all hours of every day heavy laden with nuclear armament.

Ever larger Cold War aircraft forced March to construct a new, modern air traffic control tower in the late 1960s. The bombing, refueling, and transport missions of various March units—not to mention how runways increased from 8,000 to 10,000 and finally 12,000 feet long—required infrastructure, like the tower, new maintenance facilities, and others equal to the challenge.

The Fifteenth Air Force moved to March in November 1949. Established in November 1943 in Tunisia, the Fifteenth Air Force was initially under the command of Maj. Gen. James Doolittle, a March alumnus. The members of the Fifteenth Air Force took part in every theater of America's aerial warfare from World War II to Vietnam, and today as part of the global war on terrorism, albeit with its mission moved to Scott Air Force Base, Illinois, in January 1992.

Not all missions were related to air defense, at least not directly. In 1972, a foods specialist prepares a staple of military diets in all branches. Both a brace against hunger and longing for civilian normality, fast food–style canteens remain crucial for service posts around the world.

103

In the hot zone of mission control at the Fifteenth Air Force, the board denotes daily and ongoing mission schedules, while the pilot, awaiting mission information at the end of the bank of communications equipment, wears the shield patch of Strategic Air Command. The Coke and cigarettes belie a serious, tough mission. The larger boards in the image below underscore the complicated method of keeping everything in the air in careful check.

This might have been a scene out of a sci-fi movie only 20 years before this photograph of the Fifteenth Air Force command center was taken in the mid-1980s. Overhead projectors enlarged transparencies illustrating current missions on the large screens at left while the phone bank kept in constant contact with the flight control centers and the aircraft in flight.

Gifted to March Air Force Base in 1968 by the City of Riverside, the new entrance gate off Cactus Avenue served the expanding base's updated orientation of north-south, instead of the 1932 expansion's northwest-southeast-facing layout. Bringing the story full-circle, Riverside businessmen helped trowel the first globs of mortar into place as they had half a century before.

Posing in front of the officer's club named in his honor, Gen. Henry "Hap" Arnold joins James "Jimmy" Doolittle, one of aviation's most eminent personalities, and two active duty U.S. Air Force generals. Pictured are, from left to right, an unidentified general, General Arnold, Jimmy Doolittle, and the March commander, General Mullins, in the mid-1980s.

The trees are matured, gone is the familiar checkerboard paint from the 1930s hangars, and rising are new buildings across the street from the flight line at right and water tower at bottom center in this view taken around 1969.

An unexpected snowstorm left March blanketed in clean, white snow in 1947. Aircraft, buildings, cars, and everything else was covered by a snowfall more novel than damaging, although icy conditions posed an unusual challenge to pilots used to the balmy weather March normally enjoyed. The palm trees lining the street in the image at right provide a particularly striking juxtaposition.

March Field's 22nd Bomb Wing was given the venerable B-29 Superfortress just after the close of World War II. Although forever linked with the atomic bomb and Hiroshima and Nagasaki, Japan, the B-29's finest hour was during the Korean Conflict. This 22nd Bomb Wing example, dubbed "Mission Inn" after the Riverside hotel, is pictured in Korea around 1950.

Although development of the P-80 began in the midst of World War II in 1943, operational versions of the early jet fighter were not delivered to service until the middle of 1945. Part of the 1st Fighter Wing and 67th Tactical Reconnaissance Wing, the P-80 was most valuable as a transitional aircraft, outlining the changes from traditional propeller-powered planes to much faster jets.

The B-47 Stratojet came to March in January 1953 as part of the ever dynamic and increasingly burdened 22nd Bomb Group. A decade after early American jet engines had been tested at March, the B-47 became the first aircraft of its kind on the West Coast when it appeared at the base. Although a medium-sized bomber, the B-47 still required March to obtain yet more land to build still more runway, increased from 10,000 to 12,000 feet in length. In February 1953, a KC-97 tanker of the 22nd Refueling Squadron connected mid-flight with a B-47 piloted by Maj. "Chuck" Yeager, the first such feat accomplished by the unit.

Gen. Curtis LeMay (right), the cantankerous commander of Strategic Air Command from 1948 to 1957, stands, floatation device safely donned, beneath the wing of a B-47 Stratojet at March in the early 1950s. Both the man and the plane remain icons of the Cold War aerial efforts, one for revolutionizing the U.S. Air Force's role during periods of Cold War, the other for transforming dated bombing mandates into unprecedented areas of performance.

The radar cone of a KC-135 undergoes a rainy-day inspection around 1974. After their initial arrival at March in October 1963, the KC-135 refueling aircraft served the SAC bombing mission throughout the Cold War, outliving it until at last relieved from their last mission at March in 2007.

The "City of Riverside," the first B-52 to arrive at March, occasioned a large crowd when it touched down on September 16, 1953. Signaling a new era for the U.S. Air Force, the first B-52 was soon joined by 15 others in the 2nd Bomb Squadron. The next month, the first KC-135 appeared, beginning an age where 24-hour missions were possible thanks to midair refueling.

Demonstrating just part of the enormous payloads the B-52 Stratofortress was capable of carrying, this mid-1960s event proved just how valuable a weapon the enormous bomber could be. Whether protecting Americans at home or flying dangerous missions on the other side of the world, the B-52 remains perhaps the most significant aircraft ever stationed at March. The base required $4 million worth of improvements to prepare for the arrival of the massive bomber.

Although never a rocketry base, March did enjoy the symbolic presence of a Strategic Air Command–branded Minuteman II missile, which was installed just south of the new base entrance about 1968. The missile stood as a constant reminder of the seriousness of SAC's mission along the heavily traveled base thoroughfare until it was removed to the March Field Air Museum in 1999.

*Five*

# STRENGTH IN RESERVE
## FROM DESERT STORM TO THE WAR ON TERROR
## (1991–TODAY)

The influence of Riverside's Mission Inn is still clearly seen in the buildings facing the parade grounds at the center of the 1932 major base remodeling. Perhaps most evident is this 1932 NCO quarters building: the Spanish archways, red tile roof, and plaster frieze details give immediate evidence of this historic building's heritage, reaching through time to glorify the world's greatest air power nearly a century after it was built.

The Post Theater remained in active service through much of the Cold War, closing briefly in the 1970s before reopening in 1979 as a museum dedicated to the history of March. A step in the overall preservation and revitalization effort for the historic district of March spearheaded by Gen. James Mullin, the base theater served in its museum capacity until 1981, when the displays were moved to the 1932 commissary building.

Following completion of the major remodeling and reconfiguration of March Field that had been in process since 1928, the Riverside Chamber of Commerce presented this plaque to the base in summer 1936. Installed in August of that year on a large boulder near the entrance to March Field, the plaque was later moved to a new location within the parade grounds inside the base itself, joining a collection of other plaques commemorating the servicemen, missions, and achievements of this remarkable installation.

Site of Bob Hope's very first military radio show—forerunner of his legendary USO shows—and stage for countless basketball and other friendly games throughout its many decades, the base gym is still March's main fitness center. Maintained on the exterior to match its 1930s origins, the inside is kept up-to-date with modern equipment to meet the demand of the more fitness-savvy generation of airmen and women stationed at the base.

A plaque was unveiled on the base gym in 1998 to commemorate Bob Hope's very first performance for servicemen. Now intrinsically linked with such performances, Hope did not anticipate what lay ahead when he was convinced to record his weekly NBC radio show from March in May 1941.

On May 6, 1941, Bob Hope brought his NBC radio show to the March Field gym and broadcast his national network show from this site. It marked the first time that Mr. Hope had ever performed for military personnel.

This landmark broadcast was the forerunner to the legendary USO shows that have entertained American troops around the world since 1943.

N B C

This plaque was dedicated to Bob Hope on March 28, 1998, by the Reserve Officer's Association, Chapter II, March Air Reserve Base, California.

On display along the main road in the historic district of the modern March Air Force Base, this F-4 Phantom is reminiscent of those assigned to the base's California Air National Guard. In 1987, Capt. Dean Paul "Dino" Martin, a member of the National Guard and stationed at March, was killed when he crashed his F-4 in the San Bernardino Mountains.

The park across the street from the Hap Arnold Club was dedicated to Gen. Curtis LeMay on the occasion of March's 75th anniversary. LeMay died at the March base hospital in October 1981 after residing for many years at Air Force Village West, a retirement community for veterans across the freeway from March Air Force Base.

Sally's Alley became the de rigueur hangout for servicemen of the Air Force Reserve stationed at March during the Desert Storm era. In many ways a regular neighborhood bar, albeit one on an Air Force base, Sally's Alley maintains a nostalgic atmosphere for its regular patrons, who preserve the tradition of affixing unit insignia stickers to the front door and signing the side wall in black marker.

Some things never change, though politics, strategy, weaponry, and the times might. Here officers relax and raise a glass following the close of Operation Desert Storm in the Hap Arnold Club while still an officers-only locale. A major effort directed and accomplished largely by reservists, the offensive marked a turning point in the history of March, as the base became home more and more to Air Force Reserve staff and California Air National Guard personnel.

Only the Red Cross–style motifs on the windows reveal that this was once the entrance to the base hospital, opened in 1932. Originally the doorway featured the word "Hospital" in relief. A number of officers have reported supernatural goings on in the building, especially in the basement, formerly the location of the morgue. One story involves a Medical Service Corps officer meeting an apparition of an airman in "pinks and greens," the standard dress uniform of World War II.

In their park-like setting, the buildings of the March historic district remain pristine, kept in period-correct paint schemes like these found on the firehouse.

The 1931 hangars are kept in operating condition even today, although no major aircraft in the modern Air Force can fit inside. Protected as historic structures, the hangars are among the oldest anywhere in the United States.

Built as barracks for the staff of the base hospital, this little gem of a building now serves as offices for Headquarters Fourth Air Force.

Matured and well-maintained, the March historic district is a pristine area of lush lawns on the parade grounds, shady trees, and well-kept historic buildings as beautiful today as they were nearly 80 years ago. Completed in 1996, the transformation of the aging areas of March into a historic district was a pet project of base commander Gen. James Mullin, who championed capturing the distinctive look and feel of the base c. 1932.

The chapel was added to the parade grounds district in 1941, nearly a decade after the rest of the buildings in that area were completed. Host to regular Sunday services, weddings, christenings, and memorials for 30 years before the new, much larger chapel opened in 1970, the building was restored as part of the larger historic district preservation effort in 1996.

Now used for base operations duties, the 1931 headquarters building houses information officers and is itself a shrine to March's glorious past. Inside, historic photographs and artifacts help tell the March story to visiting officials and the curious stationed on the base today.

These coveted distinguished visitor quarters for traveling officers—today called the McBride Suites—the two 1932 Bachelor Officers' Quarters (B.O.Q.) apartment garages sit just steps from the Hap Arnold Club, convenient for nights of indulgent revelry in the classic dark-wood aviators' pub.

On the modern March Air Reserve Base, the missions have changed, as have the aircraft, the buildings, and the personnel. The C-17 Globemaster has usurped the throne of the C-141 Starlifter as the base's main aircraft, along with the venerable KC-135. A modern base, up to the challenges of the modern world and grounded in a distinguished past, March is in a unique position among American air bases.

Known today as the Hap Arnold House, the 1932 base commander's house is used for receptions and parties for those stationed at the modern March Air Force Base. Inside, care has been taken to preserve the house as it looked when Arnold resided there. The house is a prime example of March leadership actively maintaining historic buildings and using them for modern-day functions. The author's grandfather mowed the lawn here as a boy when Arnold lived in the house, dreaming of his chance to take flight.

The March Field Air Museum finally got a purpose-built home in 1993 with the opening of its current location on Van Buren Boulevard, south of the base's main gate. The hangar-like main building re-creates the checkerboard roof of the 1931 March hangars. The exceptional aircraft and artifacts make the museum one of the finest aviation history collections in the United States.

Inside the March Field Air Museum, visitors will find historic aircraft and artifacts related to the story of military aviation at March and across the nation. Divided into chronological pieces of this history, the museum houses thousands of important photographs, documents, and objects from the earliest days of the base to the present.

This B-25 Mitchell stands sentry at the entrance to the March Field Air Museum. One of World War II's most instrumental aircraft, the B-25 was in use at March until 1966. The B-25 is one of more than 70 historic and modern military aircraft at the museum, including planes from throughout the 20th century. From early biplanes to warbirds like the B-25, A-26, B-17, and B-29, and modern aircraft like the SR-71, the museum's collection is almost unmatched in the world for its breadth of focus.

"Keep 'em Flying!" In 1976, on the cusp of the nation's bicentennial, Gen. Jack Catton, then the Fifteenth Air Force commander, said, "I think March AFB is one of the very most prominent bases in the United States Air Force. It has tradition. It is nearly incomparable." March Air Force Base—today's March Air Reserve Base—is certainly unique among the flying fields of our national air defense. Its tradition is incomparable. (Courtesy of the author.)

# Discover Thousands of Local History Books
## Featuring Millions of Vintage Images

Arcadia Publishing, the leading local history publisher in the United States, is committed to making history accessible and meaningful through publishing books that celebrate and preserve the heritage of America's people and places.

Find more books like this at
**www.arcadiapublishing.com**

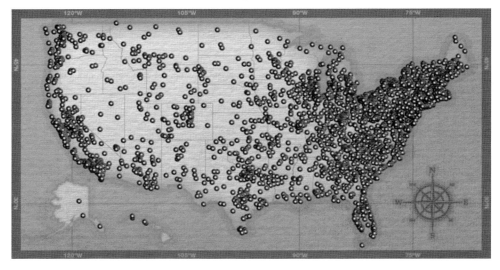

Search for your hometown history, your old stomping grounds, and even your favorite sports team.